FRUIT OF THE SPIRIT

Rose Visual Bible Studies

Fruit of the Spirit
Rose Visual Bible Studies

© 2022 Rose Publishing

Published by Rose Publishing
An imprint of Tyndale House Ministries
Carol Stream, Illinois
www.hendricksonrose.com

ISBN 978-1-4964-7397-4

All rights reserved. No part of this work may be reproduced or transmitted in any form or by any means, electronic or mechanical, including photocopying, recording, or by any information storage and retrieval system, without permission in writing from the publisher.

Author: Mary Gross Davis, Community Pastor, Saticoy Church

Scriptures taken from the Holy Bible, New International Version®, NIV®. Copyright © 1973, 1978, 1984, 2011 by Biblica, Inc.™ Used by permission of Zondervan. All rights reserved worldwide. www.zondervan.com The "NIV" and "New International Version" are trademarks registered in the United States Patent and Trademark Office by Biblica, Inc.™

Scripture quotations marked ESV are from the ESV® Bible (The Holy Bible, English Standard Version®), Copyright © 2001 by Crossway, a publishing ministry of Good News Publishers. Used by permission. All rights reserved.

Scripture quotations marked NLT are taken from the *Holy Bible*, New Living Translation, copyright © 1996, 2004, 2015 by Tyndale House Foundation. Used by permission of Tyndale House Publishers, Carol Stream, Illinois 60188. All rights reserved.

Images used under license from Shutterstock.com: mythja cover, 38, 71; leonori p. 5; SewCream pp. 3, 7; Tatevosian Yana p. 8; Art Stocker p. 9; otnaydur p. 11; songpon_peace p. 17; Song_about_summer pp. 3, 23; Shulevskyy Volodymyr pp. 24, 80; Creative Travel Projects p. 25; DRAWzdova p. 28; tomertu pp. 3, 37; Eugene Photo p. 39; New Africa p. 43; Steve Cukrov p. 44; Dmytro Zinkevych pp. 3, 51; PradaBrown p. 52; Purino p. 53; Bildagentur Zoonar GmbH p. 55; DedovStock pp. 3, 65; Anna Sedneva p. 66; by-studio p. 67; MIA Studio p. 70; Snowbelle p. 72; sarayut_sy pp. 3, 79; lovelyday12 p. 81; Josie Garner p. 83; Kazakova Maryia p. 85; Victoria Sergeeva p. 92; Chat Karen Studio pp. 3, 95; P Maxwell Photography p. 96; Amenic181 p. 99; Keep Smiling Photography 101.

Printed in the United States of America
010522VP

Contents

"But the fruit of the Spirit is love, joy, peace, patience, kindness, goodness, faithfulness, gentleness, self-control; against such things there is no law."

Galatians 5:22–23 ESV

Fruit of the Spirit

Fruit—it's something eaten by most of us! While there are those who may not like fruit (but come now, who doesn't at least like fruit *pie?*), we are all familiar with fruit. We know what it's like to bite into a perfectly ripe, juicy peach in the warmth of summer, or a tangy, crisp apple on a cool fall day. Basically, we all know that there's fruit, and then there's *fruit!*

And fruit, of course, is filled with seeds—a very tangible reminder that fruit is the product of a series of living, growing processes (miracles, in fact). Fruit seeds can sprout, grow, and create another generation of trees and plants—more peaches, more strawberries, more grapes!

Fruit can't be assembled on a conveyor belt. It's not like a manufactured product—all identical in expression. Each piece of fruit is the unique product of something living. (Skittles may be fruity and are consistently identical, but they're not fruit!)

Just after the apostle Paul's list of the fruit of the Spirit in Galatians 5, he tells his beloved fellow-believers to "keep in step with the Spirit" (verse 25). This is about walking in ways which are different from what we see around us, because it's the Holy Spirit in us, not our own "goodness," which produces this spiritual fruit. Just as Skittles aren't cherries, and lemon drops aren't lemons, genuine spiritual fruit in our lives can't be manufactured from some checklist of "spiritual fruit making." Rather, the fruit of the Spirit is the expression of the living Holy Spirit in us, growing us to spiritual maturity.

Before Paul lists the fruit of God's Spirit, he gives us another list: the deeds of "the flesh" or "sinful nature," which describe the ugly, selfish, and cruel fruit of how people act when they're not in step with God's Spirit. Paul then contrasts these behaviors and attitudes with the fruit of a life filled with the power of God's Spirit—and they're a totally opposite set of actions and attitudes.

This stark contrast should make us hunger for the powerful life-flow of God's Spirit within us. This picture in Galatians 5 is of the most luscious, peak-of-harvest spiritual fruit that not only delights and satisfies us, but also those around us. Why? Because it tastes and smells like the love of God!

It's More Than You Think

Love

How would you define the term *love*? Love is something we all talk about, a lot of the time! But it isn't often that anyone can give a clear definition of it. Movies and novels featuring love as the centerpiece are everywhere. But some give utterly misguided definitions, such as the old movie tagline: "Love means never having to say you're sorry." (What on earth does that even mean?)

Webster's Dictionary has described *love* as "a feeling of strong personal attachment induced by that which delights or commands admiration, by sympathetic understanding, or by ties of kinship; ardent affection."[1] That's good, but 1 John 3:16 gives an even better definition: "This is how we know what love is: Jesus Christ laid down his life for us. And we ought to lay down our lives for our brothers and sisters." Love is not only ardent feeling but the choice (or a series of choices) to sacrifice for another, to put another's needs ahead of our own, to lay down our lives; that means our timetables, our agendas, our expectations of that person, and more.

Love is the first thing that comes to Paul's mind as he writes out a list to the Galatians of what flows from a Spirit-empowered life: "But the fruit of the Spirit is love ..." (Galatians 5:22).

Key Bible Passages

Galatians 5:13–26 p. 1176 NT

1 Corinthians 13:1–13 p. 161 NT wedding

1 John 3:11–18 p. 219 NT

Optional Reading

Ephesians 5:1–2 p. 179 NT

1 John 3:1–3 p. 219 NT

“This is how we know what love is: Jesus Christ laid down his life for us.”

1 JOHN 3:16

Know It

1. Look at Paul's description of love in 1 Corinthians 13:4–8. List those qualities down the left side of this space. (You can use alternate words if they have more meaning for you, such as "humble" for "is not proud.") On the right side, list Paul's fruit of the Spirit from Galatians 5:22–23. What similarities do you notice?

p. 161

LOVE 1 Corinthians 13:4–8	FRUIT OF THE SPIRIT Galatians 5:22–23
patient kind not jealous not boastful not arrogant polite not irritable not resentful rejoice in the right bears all believes all hopes endures never ends/forever	love joy peace patience kindness goodness faithfulness gentleness self-control

p.

2. According to 1 John 3:11–18, what does authentic, practical love look like?

putting others before self

in deed & in truth

The Letter to the Galatians

Paul's letter was written to the churches in the region of Galatia (now part of Turkey). Earlier, Paul had traveled through Galatia, proclaiming the good news of salvation through Jesus' death and resurrection—the gift of God, entirely of his grace and not anyone's own doing. But a group, called the Judaizers, had come along behind Paul. The story they proclaimed was that without becoming converts to Judaism (obeying the Old Testament law and being circumcised) people couldn't *really* be saved. Paul's other letters (such as his letter to the Romans) make it clear that he was not in any way going to put up with this. He would not water down the astonishing grace of God to please this group who was out to discredit him and add their rules to the great message of God's grace.

In this context, Paul lays out for his beloved Galatians just what the difference is between living under the religious law (the old Jewish system) and living in the power of the Holy Spirit. Paul, a former Pharisee himself, makes it clear that he has no use for these "extras" which the Judaizers insisted were necessary for salvation. Paul points out that following religious law is not the answer for the Galatian Christians. Only by the power of the Holy Spirit would they become the people God wants them to be.

Paul supports his case in this way: He lists the acts of the flesh or sinful nature—hatred, divisions, and factions (which of course the Judaizers had created out of envy and selfish ambition), as well as things we might think of as "big sins," like idolatry, sexual promiscuity, drunkenness, and witchcraft. Paul's point is that *all* these behaviors are the outflow—or the fruit—of a life lived without the power of God's Spirit.

Outline of Galatians p. 173 - 177

1. Introduction and warnings against other gospels (1:1–10)
2. Paul's defense of his apostolic calling (1:11–2:21)
3. Justification by faith (3:1–4:31)
4. Freedom in Christ (5:1–12)
5. Living in the Spirit and the fruit of the Spirit (5:13–6:18)

> "Love is a fruit in season at all times, and within reach of every hand. Anyone may gather it and no limit is set."
>
> —Mother Teresa

WHO WROTE GALATIANS AND WHO READ IT?	The apostle Paul wrote this letter (also called an epistle) to be circulated among the churches in the region of Galatia. Paul was a devout Jew who became a Christian after encountering the risen Christ on the road to Damascus. Before this, he had violently persecuted Christians. (Read his amazing conversion story in Acts 9.)
WHERE IS GALATIA?	Galatia is in modern-day Turkey.
WHY WAS GALATIANS WRITTEN?	After Paul had left Galatia, Judaizers had come to these churches claiming that faith in Jesus was not sufficient to save them or make them right with God. They told these new believers that they had to obey Jewish law to truly follow Jesus.
WHAT IS GALATIANS ABOUT?	Galatians is Paul's rebuttal to the false teaching of the Judaizers and encouragement to the believers to remain free of the law and to follow Jesus.
WHEN WAS GALATIANS WRITTEN?	There are two possible dates. If Paul was writing to churches mostly in southern Galatia, he may have written this letter around AD 49, after his first missionary journey and just before the Jerusalem Council in Acts 15. But if Paul was writing to churches in northern Galatia, he may have written this letter around AD 54, during his stay in Ephesus on his third missionary journey.

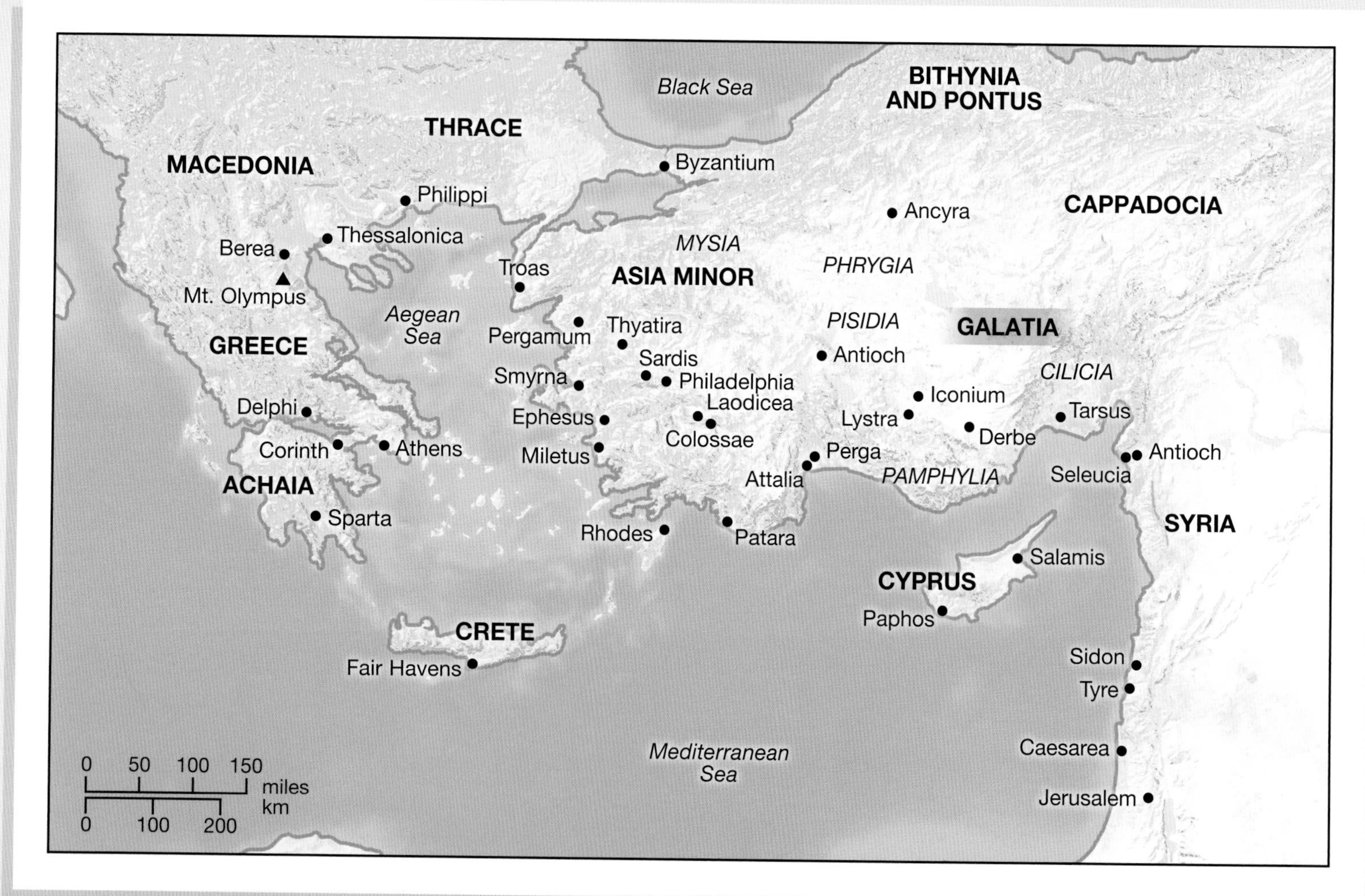
Black Sea
BITHYNIA AND PONTUS
THRACE
MACEDONIA
Byzantium
Philippi
Ancyra
CAPPADOCIA
Thessalonica
Berea
MYSIA
Troas
ASIA MINOR
PHRYGIA
Mt. Olympus
Aegean Sea
Pergamum
Thyatira
PISIDIA
GALATIA
GREECE
Sardis
Antioch
Smyrna
Philadelphia
CILICIA
Laodicea
Iconium
Delphi
Ephesus
Lystra
Tarsus
Colossae
Derbe
Corinth
Athens
Miletus
Perga
Antioch
ACHAIA
Attalia
PAMPHYLIA
Seleucia
Sparta
Rhodes
Patara
SYRIA
Salamis
CYPRUS
Paphos
CRETE
Fair Havens
Sidon
Tyre
Caesarea
Mediterranean Sea
Jerusalem
0 50 100 150 miles
0 100 200 km

The Four Loves

The New Testament uses two different words to express the concept of love: *agape* and *phileo*. Ancient Greek had four words for love with fine distinctions. Although their differences are not always clear, these words were generally used in the following ways.

AGAPE	• In Ancient Greek, *agape* was used for a general affection for people or things. • It appears over one hundred times in the New Testament. • The New Testament uses the word *agape* in a special way. It is the selfless, unconditional, deep love that Christ embodied. • *Agape* is the love that God showed for his creation (John 3:16), for Christ (John 17:26), and for those who believe in Jesus (John 14:21). • *Agape* is also the love that believers should have for each other (1 John 4:17–18).
PHILEO	• *Phileo* is not as common in the New Testament as *agape,* but it also means love. • *Phileo* refers to the affection for and response to people—such as family and friends—or activities one enjoys (John 11:3, 5; 13:23; 16:27; 1 Corinthians 16:22). • *Philadelphia* means "brotherly love" and occurs six times in the New Testament.
EROS	• This word does not appear in the New Testament. • *Eros* refers to passion and attraction between lovers, or more generally, romantic love.
STORGE	• This word does not appear in the New Testament. • *Storge* was primarily used to describe the affection between family members, for example, the natural love of parents toward children.

Live It

We all talk about love, but as Mark Twain quipped about the weather, "No one does anything about it." Love is something we all want to receive, but often it's easy to forget to give it. Some people confuse love with common interests, shared beliefs, family ties, or sexual attraction. Because wrong thinking so permeates modern society, it can be hard to know what love really is.

What Our Lord Saw from the Cross
by James Tissot

A great example of living out love is Jesus' disciple, John. Most of the intimate events surrounding Jesus' death and resurrection in the New Testament come to us because of John's eyewitness accounts in the gospel of John. The amount of detail alone indicates that John stayed with Jesus through terrifying times.

- John records Jesus' lengthy prayer on the night of his arrest (chapter 17) and the detailed questioning of Jesus at his trials (chapter 18).
- At the crucifixion, John remains with Jesus, along with a few bold and faithful women. John is apparently the only man near enough for Jesus to designate him as the new "son" of Mary (chapter 19).

- As soon as Mary Magdalene announces Jesus' resurrection, John runs to the tomb of Jesus and is the first among the disciples to reach the empty tomb (chapter 20).

John's love is not showy or dramatic; his love is sacrificial. It was proven in his constant and brave actions. So he could confidently write many years later, "Dear children, let us not love with words or speech but with actions and in truth" (1 John 3:18).

Given what Jesus did for us, and given the example of how John lived out his love for Jesus, we can see that love is more than we often think it is; it transcends sexual attraction, family relations, common interests, and intellectual bonding. Love is more than all these other "love-ish" experiences and feelings. It goes beyond the expectations and judgments we make on others. It takes us past the ways we think we should be loved or even the ways we think we should love others. This is the reason it is so deeply important to divest ourselves of wrong thinking. There is life-changing power in taking the biblical definition of love to heart!

Love

The Greek word for *love* in Galatians 5:22 is *agape*, pronounced ah-GAH-pey. The underlying essence of *agape* is a supremely self-sacrificing love. It occurs more than one hundred times in the New Testament.[2]

Life Application Questions

1. How does the kind of love Jesus demonstrates seem different from what you might see in pop culture and the media, or what you were "taught" in your family, schools, or even in churches?

passion - rom coms

media - fake love, popularity

truly caring

Jesus' love is unconditional

should be deep + not easily broken

2. At this point in your life, what's your definition of love? Has it changed over the years? If so, how?

deeply caring - not easily broken

long term game

commitment + duty

3. John describes God's love as being *lavished* upon us (1 John 3:1). What is one way you've seen or felt the lavish love of God in your life?

Dad / family.

God's love always "walking" with us whether we realize it or not

1/17

4. In what ways have you seen another person love sacrificially, in the "Jesus way"? What did that person do to lay down his or her life, agenda, or expectations to show love?

5. What are some things that keep people from loving others well?

6. Think of a person in your life who is difficult to love. What are two things you could do to show him or her love in a positive, noticeable, Jesus-like way? (And avoidance is not an option!)

Fruitful Activation

Let's bite a little deeper into this fruit and savor it longer. Here, at the end of each session, you'll find activities that you can do on your own or with your small group to reflect upon and cultivate the fruit of the Spirit. Here are some ideas:

- Browse today's news headlines. See if you can find a story of a person who has either loved or hated, and look for clues for what attitudes and events led to his or her actions.
- Take some time to read or listen with an audio Bible to the arrest, crucifixion, and resurrection account found in John 17–20. Think about the actions of John and Jesus. Imagine what it must have been like to be one of those who stood by Jesus at the cross. How much love do you think it would take to "stand with" Jesus as he is being tortured and killed on the cross, knowing that by being with him you're making yourself available for death as well?
- Take another look at your answer for Life Application Question #6. Now commit to taking those steps toward showing that hard-to-love person "Jesus love." What will you do in the coming week to make this happen?

Notes

2 JOY & PEACE

The Inside Job

Joy & Peace

Joy! Peace! The very words bring a sense of well-being, of relaxation in a setting of emotional positivity. But before we sink too deeply into that lovely feeling, let's go back to our friendly dictionary to be sure we know what we're talking about. Webster's dictionary has defined *joy* as "the emotion excited by the acquisition or expectation of good; pleasurable feelings caused by a sense of well-being, success, good fortune, and the like;" and *peace* as "a state of quiet or tranquility; freedom from disturbance or agitation; harmony between individuals; freedom from personal strife or quarrels."

These next two fruits of the Spirit in Paul's list are certainly an "inside job." Joy and peace must grow inside of us first before they are expressed on the outside. This kind of joy and peace that the Bible talks about can't be legislated, decreed, manufactured, or forced upon people.

Those who are at peace and who possess joy are best suited to help others receive them. When one is surrounded by people who are in joyless dispeace, the fruits of joy and peace become like superpowers! They are powerful fruits to share with those who are hungry for tranquility and well-being. As we keep in step with the Spirit, we find that these two fruits grow on the inside so that we can share them with others on the outside.

Key Bible Passages

Isaiah 55:6–13 p. 647 OT

Philippians 4:4–9 p. 183 NT

Optional Reading

John 14:1–31 p. 101 NT

“You will go out in joy and be led forth in peace; the mountains and hills will burst into song before you.”

ISAIAH 55:12

1. Isaiah 55:6–13 gives us a snapshot of what life can look like when people have turned from sin and are ready to receive God's peace (verse 7). Jot down all the imagery from creation that you can find used in this passage to depict a joy-filled and peace-full world.

mercy
be pardoned (abundantly)
~~reknown~~

2. In Isaiah 55:13, what is the reason given for these great blessings and the flourishing of beauty where thorns had grown before?

Lord - as a memorial
reknown - forever

3. In your own words, how would you describe the kind of peace that "transcends" or "surpasses" all understanding (Philippians 4:7)?

grace + peace of JC
not earthly
unexplanable

Shalom

On the heels of love in Paul's fruit of the Spirit list comes the back-to-back fruits of joy and peace. Why treat these two together? Well, consider this: Have you ever had joy without peace? Peace without joy? These two feed off each other and sustain each other. They are living expressions of the love of God which flows into our lives—and then out through our lives.

In fact, the Hebrew word *shalom* found in the Old Testament, which we think of as "peace," has a meaning which encompasses joy as well. Cornelius Plantinga in his book *Not the Way It's Supposed to Be* describes the concept of *shalom* as follows:

> The webbing together of God, humans, and all creation in justice, fulfillment, and delight is what the Hebrew prophets call *shalom*. We call it peace, but it means far more than mere peace of mind or a cease-fire between enemies. In the Bible, *shalom* means *universal flourishing, wholeness and delight*—a rich state of affairs in which natural needs are satisfied and

Joy

The Greek word for *joy* in Galatians 5:22 is *chara*, pronounced KAH-rah. Also translated as *gladness*, *chara* is used in the New Testament as the experience of receiving God's Word, his power, and the Holy Spirit. It's a fruit of the Spirit in the lives of those who partake of the kingdom of God and the resurrection. It's derived from the verb *chairo,* which means "rejoice." *Chara* occurs about sixty times in the New Testament.

natural gifts fruitfully employed, a state of affairs that inspires joyful wonder as its Creator and Savior opens doors and welcomes the creatures in whom he delights. *Shalom*, in other words, is the way things ought to be.[3]

It has been said that doing God's will is following that sweet spot of peace which is the Holy Spirit. Imagine how our lives might change by living centered in that joyful *shalom*. Remember Paul's admonition to "keep in step with the Spirit" (Galatians 5:25)? It's the key—and then joy and peace can flow, regardless of one's circumstances.

"If God be our God, he will give us peace in trouble. When there is a storm without, he will make peace within. The world can create trouble in peace, but God can create peace in trouble."

—Thomas Watson

Joy + Peace + Thankfulness

Throughout the Bible, there seems to be a consistent connection between thankfulness, joy, and peace. As we praise God, we remember who he is and what he has already done for us. This helps us be centered not only on the reason we are praying, but also on the character of the One to whom we pray. When we endure troubled times, praise and thanks change our perspective and refocus us on God—instead of on the problem.

Philippians 4:6–9 lays out the formula in detail:

1. First, choose not to worry about *anything*.

   "Do not be anxious about anything ..." (verse 6)

2. Then, pray about *everything*.

   "... but in every situation, by prayer and petition" (verse 6)

3. And pray with thanksgiving.

   "... with thanksgiving, present your requests to God." (verse 6)

Peace

The Greek word for *peace* in Galatians 5:22 is *eirene,* pronounced eh-REY-ney. The idea of *eirene* is very similar to the Old Testament Hebrew word *shalom.* Like *shalom, eirene* can be a blessing, greeting, or state of wholeness and tranquility. In the New Testament, it is something given by God through Christ. The gospel message is a "gospel of peace" (Ephesians 6:15). *Eirene* occurs about ninety times in the New Testament.

4. The result? God's peace, which is beyond description and past understanding, will guard our heart and mind.

   "And the peace of God, which transcends all understanding, will guard your hearts and your minds in Christ Jesus." (verse 7)

5. Choose what to think—choosing thoughts about what is good. It's a prescription for peace, joy, and mental wellness!

   "... whatever is true, whatever is noble, whatever is right, whatever is pure, whatever is lovely, whatever is admirable—if anything is excellent or praiseworthy—think about such things." (verse 8)

6. Finally, trust that the God of peace is always with you.

   "... and the God of peace will be with you." (verse 9)

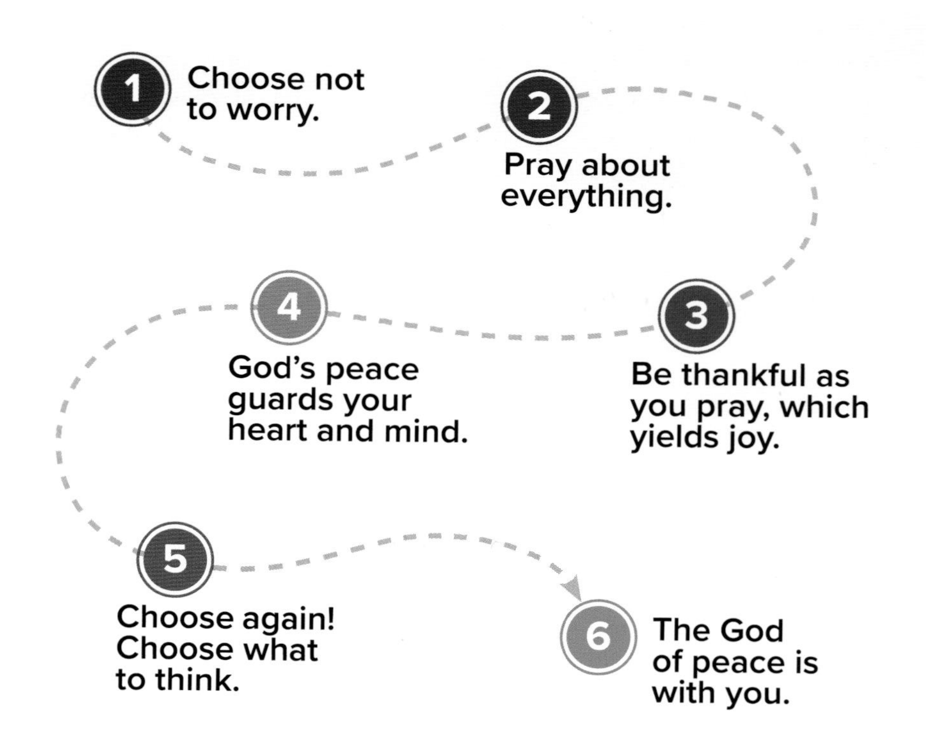

Live It

As said in the outset of this session, joy can be defined as that feeling of an "expectation of good." When we bring to the Lord all our worries and all those things that cause us dispeace, we wait on him, trusting that he will show up. But it's not about putting expectations on God: "This must be the way God will show up!" It's about waiting with a sense of expectancy: "God will show up here!"

Oswald Chambers, in his famous devotional *My Utmost for His Highest,* explains expectancy like this:

> Do not look for God to come in a particular way, but do look for Him. The way to make room for Him is to expect Him to come, but not in a certain way.... Gracious uncertainty is the mark of the spiritual life.... To be certain of God means that we are uncertain in all our ways, we do not know what a day may bring forth. This is generally said with a sigh of sadness, it should be rather an expression of breathless expectation. We are uncertain of the next step, but we are certain of God. Immediately we abandon to God, and do the duty that lies nearest. He packs our life with surprises all the time.... Leave the whole thing to Him, it is gloriously uncertain how He will come in, but He will come.[4]

"Joy is the serious business of heaven."

—C. S. Lewis

Life Application Questions

1. What does joy mean to you? Is it the same as happiness?

joy - internal long-lasting

happiness - external more temporary

joy = share it

happiness = more selfish

joy = unconditional

happiness = got something

2. Paul says that the acts of the flesh or sinful nature include discord, dissensions, and factions (Galatians 5:20). What things are necessary for a community (like a church, class, or neighborhood) to move from strife to a place of peace?

1/31

communication

find common ground + purpose

establish some "rules"

be kind to each other

don't look at others' faults

put others' above self

forgiveness!!!

3. What might it look like to put aside our expectations of God and instead wait on him with expectancy? Give an example.

(related to David's sermon on Jan. 28)?

prayerful
patience (next unit)
calmly waiting

4. How might confident prayer and giving thanks before we see God's response to our prayers set us up for joy and peace?

give thanks & count blessings before asking for anything or complaining

bends & opens your heart to blessings
lifting a weight off you
trust Him - He is looking out for our best interests

5. Have you ever experienced the God-given peace that transcends all understanding? If so, what was that like? Did it change how you viewed God or your circumstances?

calm
not as many nerves
resolute

6. Think of a time when you intentionally thanked and praised God for what he has done. What was the effect? Were you more joyful or peaceful? Maybe it's time to stop what you're doing and thank God right now.

definitely more peaceful
nerves went away

intentional
blessed

Fruitful Activation

- Draw some fun, fruitful pictures. Draw a picture of your favorite fruit, one that gives you joy to eat. Draw another picture of a fruit that you might associate with peace or one which makes you feel calm. The quality of the art doesn't matter; this is just for the creative experience. And remember the admonition of Bob Ross, the TV painting teacher: There are no mistakes, just happy accidents.
- Over the next five days read these five psalms: Psalms 146–150. Each of these hallelujah psalms begins with the joyful refrain, "Praise the LORD!"
- Thanksgiving isn't just for the holidays. At a meal with family or a gathering of your Bible study group, invite each member to describe a circumstance he or she is in—good or bad, or somewhere in between. Then take a moment for all to join together to give thanks to God in that circumstance. Praise God ahead of time for the ways in which he might work.

Notes

3 PATIENCE & FAITHFULNESS

It's Worth the Wait

Patience & Faithfulness

Patient and *faithful* sound like names for a pair of old horses, don't they! They're not glamorous names like Beauty or Champion. But they are the beautiful fruit of God's presence in our lives that make us spiritual champions.

Patience and faithfulness aren't qualities that come naturally to most people. Because we live in a world where so much is about getting "what I want, when I want, and I want it now," cultivating these two Holy Spirit fruits will get you noticed—or better yet, get Jesus noticed through you.

As these two fruits of the Spirit flow both into us and then through us, God's love will be powerfully exhibited over the long haul of life.

Read It

Key Bible Passage

Exodus 14:1–31 OT p. 59-60

Optional Reading

Colossians 1:9–12

Hebrews 10:22–25

James 5:7–9

> "See how the farmer waits for the land to yield its valuable crop, patiently waiting for the autumn and spring rains. You too, be patient and stand firm."
>
> JAMES 5:7–8

Know It

1. Look again at the Israelites' words to Moses in Exodus 14:11–12. Write out one or more beliefs they express about God. Where do they seem to put their faith?

they would have rather stayed in Egypt as slaves than die in the wilderness

2. What does Moses say in his reply (verses 13–14)?

fear not, be strong
God will fight for you - be still (patient)

3. If the Israelites had not waited for God to place the cloud between them and the Egyptians, or had not waited for the Red Sea to part, what do you think might have happened?

would have died or been returned to slavery

Beautiful Patience

Webster's Dictionary has defined patience as "calm endurance, especially under suffering or provocation." Most of us associate patience with waiting: sitting in a doctor's office, standing in line at the grocery store, taking a number at a crowded deli counter—or at the dreaded DMV! We live within this social contract of "taking turns." (This is true of most Western cultures but taking turns doesn't look the same in every society.)

But there is another type of patience. We know that in order to produce something beautiful—whether a sculpture, a handmade cello, even a newborn baby—those processes require patience, a kind of focused diligence, a way of thinking about and being absorbed in that process without irritation or rancor. We recognize instinctively that some things are worth the wait—and we then act accordingly.

Some Bible versions translate the Greek word for patience (*makrothumia*) as *forbearance*. Maybe this is because forbearance carries with it the idea of *not* doing something one *might* do while waiting—like grumbling, fuming, or flying off the handle.

Patience

The Greek word for *patience* in Galatians 5:22 is *makrothumia,* pronounced mah-krow-THEW-me-ah. Literally, it means "long temper" or, as we might say today, having a long fuse. In some Bible versions, it is translated as *forbearance* or *longsuffering*. It occurs fourteen times in the New Testament.

Forbearance is closely related to patience in the sense that it keeps us from doing or saying something we might regret.

Henri Nouwen, the Dutch theologian and thinker, paints this beautiful picture of patience:

> Patience asks us to live the moment to the fullest, to be completely present to the moment, to taste the here and now, to be where we are. When we are impatient we try to get away from where we are. We behave as if the real thing will happen tomorrow, later and somewhere else. Let's be patient and trust that the treasure we look for is hidden in the ground on which we stand.[5]

Fearless Faithfulness

It's common to think of faithfulness as doing the same thing the same way over a long period of time. This is valuable, but the motivation for this behavior is what makes the difference. Some people are consistent over time simply because they are afraid to do otherwise or are just in a rut. But faithfulness isn't a rut. An early edition of Webster's Dictionary has defined faithfulness as "full of faith; believing, especially in the promises of God" and "a firm adherence to promises, true and constant in affection and allegiance, and worthy of confidence or belief." It's being full

Faithfulness

The Greek word for *faithfulness* in Galatians 5:22 is *pistis,* pronounced PISS-tiss. Also translated simply as *faith*, this word carries with it the idea of belief, trust, confidence, and conviction. It occurs over two hundred times in the New Testament.

of faith that causes a fearless, unfailing response to life's ups and downs.

But rather than cite a theologian about this, let me tell you about a big dog named Jake. He taught me a great deal about being faithful. Although he was faithfully (predictably) at the door when I came home, his faithfulness was best expressed when he would lie at the end of the kitchen, watching me cook. He didn't whine or beg. He was so completely full of faith in me, so fully believing that I would do him good and toss him any worthy scrap, that he was content to wait quietly. His steady confidence that I was good and would be good to him was the basis of his faith. Such faith is irresistibly charming. And of course, he always got delectable scraps!

Our loving Father in heaven cares for us far more than anyone could ever love their dog. As Scripture reminds us, he prepares a banquet (not scraps!) for us with all the choicest foods (Isaiah 25:6–8). He is eager to do "immeasurably more than all we ask or imagine" (Ephesians 3:20) when we choose to be full of faith in him—faith-full! We are willing to wait restfully because our faith is in the One who always keeps his promises.

Old Faithful

There is a famous geyser in Yellowstone National Park affectionately named Old Faithful. Park naturalists can predict with a 90 percent confidence rate the time of the next eruption, plus or minus ten minutes. In the summer, crowds gather to see the earth "let off steam," up to over eight thousand gallons of water! And they usually don't have to wait long. Old Faithful erupts about twenty times a day.

In spite of its name, Old Faithful isn't perfectly on schedule. You can't set your watch by its eruptions. But what naturalists have found over the past years is that Old Faithful is consistent, given the parameters of what's going on under the surface of the earth on any given day (which they can't see). It might erupt a bit earlier or later; since an earthquake in 1959, it now erupts one time less per day than it did before. Yet you can count on it happening, even though it may not be according to your schedule. Old Faithful is still faithful.

The crowds at Yellowstone don't know precisely how high the water will shoot up or exactly when, but they gather to wait for Old Faithful because they are faithful too. They believe that the nature of Old Faithful is to erupt consistently—on its own timetable.

We don't know exactly how or when God will show up in a particular situation in our life, but we come and wait patiently, faithfully with the expectancy that our faithful God will arrive. And God's timing is always worth the wait!

Live It

When you pray, what's your attitude as you approach God, your loving Father?

- Do you try to get him to worry with you?
- Do you complain or whine to him?
- Do you try to give him advice, as if you know how the matter ought to be handled?
- Or do you focus on his character, anticipate his goodness, and thank him for what he will do?

Like it or not, our prayers express the level of our faithfulness—or faith-filled-ness. When we are convinced that he is good and truly know that he loves us, we can give ourselves permission to wait, quietly alert, expectant for him to do what is best. Otherwise, we look to other things to trust: our own ability, money, significant others, political leaders. These easily become our idols, because an idol is anything we trust in place of God—a kind of a Plan B if God doesn't come through.

> "[Patience is] a grace as difficult as it is necessary, and as hard to come [by] as it is precious when it is gained."
>
> —Charles Spurgeon

Idolatry is what makes us faith*less* people in God's eyes. It's living proof that we are in step with the flesh ("I've got to do something about this!") instead of the Spirit ("Be still and know that I am God"). It may be the hardest thing we have ever done, but it's the essence of faithfulness: letting God be God.

Remember Paul's list of the works of the flesh in Galatians 5? Our temptation may not be to physically kill a person, but we may be tempted to kill a reputation or to take matters into our own hands. But Paul considers selfish ambition and creating division to be just as much works of the flesh as sexual immorality or carousing—not something we usually hear in church, but it's biblical truth!

The Holy Spirit within us enables us to have patience when we've run out of it, and to be faithful even when our fear overtakes our trust. As we keep in step with the Spirit, we discover that our fuse is longer and our calmness lingers, and we may be amazed to hear ourselves speaking words of encouragement from a heart of rest.

"He is not just *a* faithful God but the faithful God. He is the same steadfast and good Father yesterday, today, and forever."

—JONI EARECKSON TADA

Life Application Questions

1. Read Hebrews 10:22. What do you think it means for us to draw near to God with full assurance? What should we have full assurance of?

2. When have you seen another person be full of faith in God? What actions showed you his or her faith and what effect did it have on you?

3. When in your past has God faithfully kept his promise to you? Describe a specific event.

4. What do you feel is your biggest roadblock to trusting God completely?

5. How can you show patience with those you live with? Those you work with? Those you go to school or church with?

6. What are some practices or habits that help you keep in step with the Spirit of God, growing in patience and faithfulness?

Fruitful Activation

- Read or listen from an audio Bible to the story in 2 Chronicles 20:1–30. Think about the steps Jehoshaphat took when tremendous danger came. Imagine yourself in that square, terrified yet worshiping with the Israelites. Notice the core of the king's prayer (verses 6–12), and how the people responded to God's answer through a prophet. What actions proved their faith in God?
- On the surfaces of a blank take-out container, write or illustrate your "take outs" from this session. What have you learned about patience and faithfulness? Or, you could write your "take outs" on slips of paper and put them in the container; then pull out one slip each day and read it to remind yourself of a truth about patience or faithfulness.
- Eugene Peterson's book *A Long Obedience in the Same Direction: Discipleship in an Instant Society* is a great read if you want to spend more time considering how to patiently and faithfully live out God's love over the long haul of life.

Notes

The Universal Language of Grace

Kindness

"Be nice!" We've probably all heard moms or dads shout those two words at kids who are not playing well together. *Nice* means to be pleasant, agreeable, or polite; it carries a sense of social reciprocity: "Be nice to me, and I'll be nice to you." But is being nice the same as being kind?

Kindness—Paul's fifth spiritual fruit on his list—goes deeper than being pleasant or agreeable. Its synonyms are *gracious, benevolent, considerate,* and *loving*. Those are all words which could describe God. A gracious response of heart-level benevolence—regardless of what we expect the other person to do for us—goes beyond being nice. In Luke 6, Jesus lays out the details of this idea: He told his followers to "do good to those who hate you" and "pray for those who mistreat you." That's the power of kindness: it actively gives grace, goodness, or blessing where there is no expectation of receiving them in return.

This is not behavior we often see in our "me first" culture—even among "nice" people. But genuine kindness is truly revolutionary! It speaks a universal language because it is a literal, practical expression of God's grace.

Read It

Key Bible Passages

Matthew 25:31–46

Luke 6:27–36 p. 59 NT

Optional Reading

Micah 6:8

1 Corinthians 13:4

Ephesians 4:32

Colossians 3:12–13

"As God's chosen people, holy and dearly loved, clothe yourselves with compassion, kindness ..."

COLOSSIANS 3:12

Know It

1. In the parable of the sheep and goats, what are the six things that the sheep do, and the goats do not?

   1. ______________________________

   2. ______________________________

   3. ______________________________

   4. ______________________________

   5. ______________________________

   6. ______________________________

2. In Jesus' teaching in Luke 6:27–36, which of the actions described is the most challenging for you?

3. If you did the optional reading for this session, look for words in those verses that mean something similar to kindness and write them down. Consider how these words differ or are alike.

Explore It

The Parable of the Sheep and Goats

In the Matthew 25:31–46, Jesus describes separating people gathered before him as a shepherd would separate sheep from goats. The actions of the "sheep" are considered as being done to Jesus himself, and these people are called righteous (verse 37). Did their kind deeds make them righteous? (That would contradict Paul's teaching in Galatians, wouldn't it? See Galatians 3.) No, their actions done on the outside prove their inner condition of righteousness. The righteous person is righteous because of Jesus' death and resurrection, when he exchanged our unrighteousness for his righteousness. It's our relationship with him that gives us inner resources to act in ways that reveal the righteousness given by Christ.

Let's note the situation of those in need in this parable:

- **Hunger and Thirst**

  Think of a time when you fed a person who could never invite you to dinner or pay you back in any way. Have you ever given water to a stranger simply because the person was thirsty? What transpired? How did that affect you?

- **Being an Outsider**

  What do you remember most about a time when you chose to make a stranger into a friend? When have you invited a person into your home, your church group, or your circle of friends whom you hardly knew? What was the most difficult and risky part of that? What was the most rewarding?

- **Needing Clothes and Medical Care**

  Clothing donations and money given to medical ministries, even transporting people to doctor appointments or nursing a sick person are all acts of kindness. When have you done these things, and how did it affect your heart or attitude? What do you think it did for the recipients?

- **Imprisoned**

  Prisoners are the people most often aware of their need of both human compassion and of Jesus. Sadly, they're also often the most forgotten by the outside world. Have you ever visited someone in prison? What resulted from that visit?

Notice that the "goats" in Jesus' parable didn't rob any banks or shoot up a neighborhood. They simply expressed their inner condition—their essential selfishness—through their inaction. They didn't bother to reach out to the hungry, the outsider, the sick, or the imprisoned. Jesus considers even the smallest, selfless types of humble, kind acts to be hallmarks of our relationship with him—our inner condition.

Kindness

The Greek word for *kindness* in Galatians 5:22 is *chrestotes,* pronounced krey-STAH-teys. It is used both to refer to God's kindness shown to humankind through Jesus Christ and the kindness believers show to one another. It occurs ten times in the New Testament.

The Story of Naomi

While Ruth may be the protagonist in the Old Testament book of Ruth, it's Naomi's transformation in this story that's truly remarkable. In the narrative, Naomi loses her husband and both her sons when they lived for many years in a foreign land. Widowed and very poor, she returns to her small hometown of Bethlehem with only her foreign daughter-in-law Ruth by her side. In fact, Naomi is so distraught that she blames God for her situation and changes her name from Naomi, which means "pleasant," to Mara, which means "bitter" (Ruth 1:20).

Naomi and Ruth
by Evelyn De Morgan (1887)

The Hebrew word *hesed* shows up several times in the book of Ruth. In the Old Testament, *hesed* is a rich, full word translated into English as kindness, mercy, steadfast love, or lovingkindness. *Hesed* is not about just being nice or polite; it's a type of loyal love intertwined with kindness and mercy. In the story, Naomi is shown *hesed* by Ruth who sticks by her mother-in-law, taking care of her every step of the way. The landowner, Boaz, shows *hesed* to both Ruth and Naomi, securing food, status, and property for the widows. Through their kindness, Naomi comes to recognize the Lord's kindness (Ruth 2:20). By the end of the book, Naomi's bitter life is redeemed and renewed because "the LORD … has not left [her]" (Ruth 4:14–15).

This short, wonderful story tucked into the Old Testament reminds us that the Lord's steadfast, lovingkindness—his *hesed*—is often demonstrated through the kindness of the people he brings into our lives and the kindness we can show to others when they need it most.

Live It

Jesus makes it clear that our calling is to be kind in the same way our Father in heaven is kind—indiscriminately! That sounds impossible. But in the words of Thomas Merton, "Our job is to love others without stopping to inquire whether or not they are worthy. That is not our business and, in fact, it is nobody's business. What we are asked to do is to love, and this love itself will render both ourselves and our neighbors worthy if anything can."[6]

While this sounds like a great concept, how do we love indiscriminately?

Let's consider this by looking at another use of the English word *kind*. When we are with close friends or family, with those who are similar to us, who look like us and talk like us, we might say we are "with our own kind." As birds of a feather flock together, we humans, too, are usually most comfortable around those like us. If we are honest, most of us aren't eager to meet and bless people who upset us, disagree with us, or just make us feel awkward. But it is in spending time with and listening to those who are not like us—not our "kind"—that we learn the lavish, indiscriminate kindness of God, who is kind to all.

> "Often the only thing a child can remember about an adult in later years, when he or she is grown, is whether or not that person was kind to him or her."
>
> —BILLY GRAHAM

Life Application Questions

1. What are some things in society that hinder people from behaving with kindness toward one another—or make unkindness just too easy?

2. Look again at the specific acts of kindness in the parable of the sheep and goats. What acts of kindness might you add to this list for our twenty-first century world?

3. When Jesus says to "be merciful, just as your Father is merciful" (Luke 6:36), what does it means to show mercy to "your enemies" (Luke 6:27)?

remember where you come from

being merciful = turn the other check

line between mercy + passivity?

4. Finish the following sentences:

"Being kind to my family means ...

loving unconditionally

____."

"Being kind to my friends means ...

____

____."

"Being kind to my neighbors means ...

____

____."

"Being kind to strangers means ...

____

____."

5. How might our desire for being around those who make us comfortable (our "kind") limit what God has in store for us? What might you miss out on?

variety

turn into what God wants us to

new perspective

could be an opportunity to see what God wants us to do.

6. What are some ways you can step out of your comfort zone to get to know people who are different from you?

don't stay at home

notice others

volunteer time and/or talents

Fruitful Activation

- Read the story of Ruth or listen to it with an audio Bible. It's only four short chapters in the Old Testament, but it packs a powerful kindness punch. Consider how lovingkindness (*hesed*) weaves its way through the narrative.
- Challenge yourself this week to do one "kind as God is kind" act every day. It may simply be smiling at someone you pass on the street, holding a door open to let another go first, saying "bless you" when someone sneezes, or telling a cashier she is doing a great job. Write down what happens, just so you have a record for yourself. These little acts can be powerful expressions of that indiscriminate kindness that flows from God's love. All of humankind needs to be seen, appreciated, and encouraged!

Notes

Notes

5 GOODNESS

The Power of Consistency

Goodness

It's all good. Good times! That's a good burger. She looks good.

The concept of goodness can be fuzzy. It's used in so many ways. But as a fruit of God's Spirit, goodness might seem even more elusive, like an overly-spiritual, halo-wearing quality—something "out there" we can wish for but never get to. So what does *good* really mean?

While a dictionary may tell us that it's related to being pleasing, acceptable, or appropriate ("a good burger"), it can also mean the quality of being morally right ("a good guy").

But when a rich young ruler addressed Jesus, calling him "good teacher," Jesus replied, "Why do you call me good? No one is good—except God alone" (Luke 18:19). The young man had reduced *good* to a flattering greeting. Jesus' response defined *good* further—and his definition stops us in our tracks. He pointed out that goodness is not just a nice word. Goodness, in the Jesus sense, is a very high calling indeed. This kind of goodness is only available to those in whom God's Spirit resides. That's why goodness makes its way onto Paul's list of spiritual fruits.

Read It

Key Bible Passage

Luke 18:15–30 p. 75 NT

Optional Reading

Exodus 33:19 p. 78 OT

Psalm 23:6 p. 485 OT

Ephesians 5:5–10 p. 179- OT

> "The fruit of the light consists in all goodness, righteousness, and truth."
>
> EPHESIANS 5:9

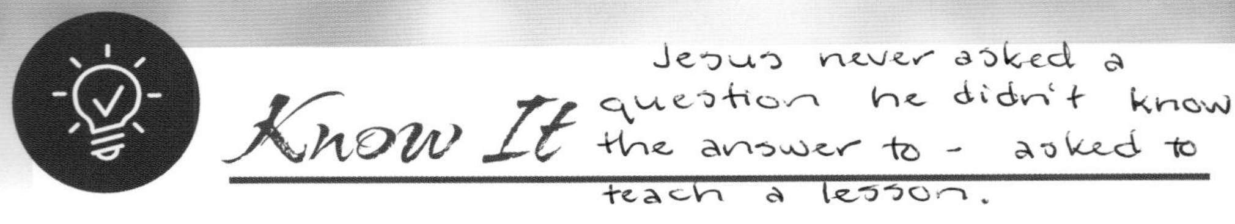

Know It

1. Why do you think Jesus questioned the rich young ruler for addressing him as "good teacher"?

2. To some, the young man's wealth might have been seen as proof that he was a "good guy." After all, God was blessing him with riches, right? Do you think his wealth was a blessing or a curse—or both?

3. Consider the characters in Luke 18:15–30. Of all the people, whom does the kingdom of God belong?

Uncomplicated Goodness

Notice in Luke 18 what Jesus said about children who had been dismissed by adults as unimportant:

> Let the little children come to me, and do not hinder them, for the kingdom of God belongs to such as these. Truly I tell you, anyone who will not receive the kingdom of God like a little child will never enter it. (verses 16–17)

Let's think about what Jesus is saying here: There is a simplicity, purity, and humble dependence in a young child that is beautiful to see. Like in the story of the rich young man—who was sure he was a "good guy" because he'd kept the law—goodness doesn't come from checking boxes on our spiritual "to do" list. The man had checked all the boxes he knew to check—except for one: he couldn't let go of his wealth. "How hard it is for the rich to enter the kingdom of God!" (Couldn't you just see Jesus shaking his head as he says this.) "Indeed, it is easier for a camel to go through the eye of a needle than for someone who is rich to enter the kingdom of God" (Luke 18:24–25).

Goodness

The Greek word for *goodness* in Galatians 5:22 is *agathosune,* pronounced ah-GAH-thow-SOO-ney. In the New Testament, *good* (*agathos*) and *goodness* occur nearly one hundred times and can mean moral uprightness, the ultimate spiritual benefit, well-being, high quality, health, virtuousness, and right living.

Although the man may have longed to be like a child again, pure and uncomplicated, he loved the riches he relied upon. To him, his wealth was a chief good in life. That love kept him from a childlike state of dependence, simplicity, and freedom that comes with life in Jesus. He went away with his worldly wealth intact—and his longing unsatisfied.

How does this relate to goodness? The spiritual fruit of goodness isn't good impulses or occasional good deeds. It's the outgrowth of God's Spirit within us as we remain in humble, childlike dependence on him. It is his work within and through us, not some spiritual exercise to do or a list we complete. Goodness is the result—the fruit—of submitting to Jesus and relying on him for every answer. It is in the soil of full dependence that the fruit of goodness grows strong over time. In childlike reliance on the Lord, this kind of deep-seated, other-centered, lifelong goodness grows.

Living in the Kingdom of God

There are more than one hundred references in the New Testament to the kingdom of God or kingdom of heaven. Jesus announced that God's kingdom was at hand, nearby, and about to come (Mark 1:15).

So what is this kingdom?

Here is a simple way to think of it: If there's a kingdom, then there must be a king. God is the king. Jesus said he is the way into God's kingdom (John 14:6). This kingdom is God's realm and reign over the lives of those who willingly submit to him as king. All those who have trusted in Jesus for salvation are people who belong to God's kingdom.

Life in this kingdom looks radically different from life according to the world's kingdom. Here are just a few examples:

THE WORLD SAYS ...	JESUS SAYS ...
Strive for earthly wealth (Mark 4:19).	Focus on heavenly treasures (Matthew 6:19–20).
Hate your enemies (Matthew 5:43).	Love your enemies and do good to those who hate you (Luke 6:27).
Be confident in your own goodness and good deeds (Luke 18:9–12).	Ask God for mercy and rely on his goodness (Luke 18:13–14).
Judge the imperfections of others and ignore your own (Matthew 7:3).	Look honestly at your own faults (Matthew 7:5).

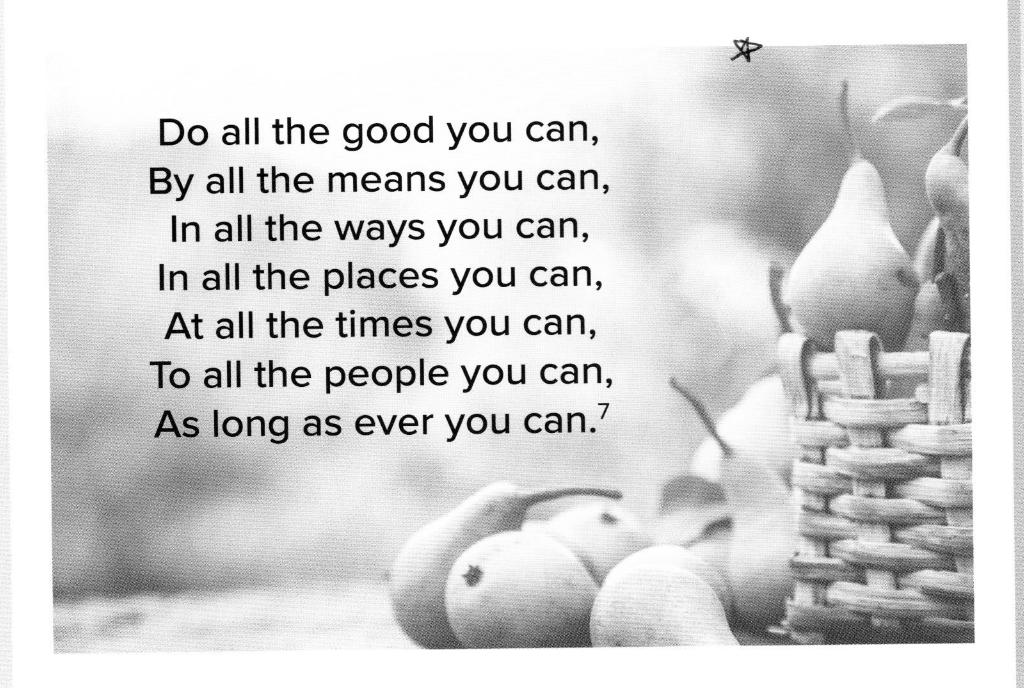

Goodness—All the Way Through

Someone who was a chocolate aficionado once gave this description of goodness: She said, "Oh! It's like chocolate! One hundred percent, pure good all the way through!" In other words, there was nothing in that chocolate to keep it from being purely delightful to her. She could rely on it being good, no matter where she bit into it.

Did you know that the country of France has strict laws about what ingredients are allowed in the chocolate produced there? They take good chocolate seriously! Their rules focus on the quality of the ingredients and on the purity and consistency of the finished product. This chocolate is more costly than lesser kinds, which may use moldy beans or be filled with skim milk or hydrogenated fats. But these differences have made French chocolate world-famous!

Consistency is what makes the spiritual fruit of goodness so powerful. It's got a quality and purity that never falters, all the way through.

Can We Have Goodness without God?

Good deeds aren't only done by followers of Jesus. That's true. Anyone can do a good deed. But here's the difference: although many people have good impulses or do good deeds, Jesus' focus is on the motive.

A person may do a good deed …

- out of a sense of duty: "I ought to this."
- from fear of punishment: "If I don't do this, I'm going to get in trouble."
- to get something in return: "If I do this, then I'm sure to get something good back."
- from a desire to gain recognition: "I hope my video showing my good deed goes viral."

But as we keep in step with God's Holy Spirit, he gives us the staying power that takes us beyond spotty, good actions into a life of real and consistent goodness. He works in our hearts to change our motivations. It's a lifelong journey to grow this goodness fruit, with lots of ups and downs along the way, but God will sprout goodness in us and bring it to its full beauty and flavor when we keep in step with the Spirit.

Life Application Questions

1. Below are some character traits related to goodness. Finish each expression and think through what it means to be good.

Generosity = good at giving

Graciousness = good at being thankful / kind / compassionate

Honesty = good at being trusted / trustworthy / admitting faults

Integrity = good at keeping your word / doing right / moral principles

Mercy = good at forgiving / being compassionate

Rightness = good at telling right from wrong

Simplicity = good at being content with life

What does the spiritual fruit of goodness mean to you?

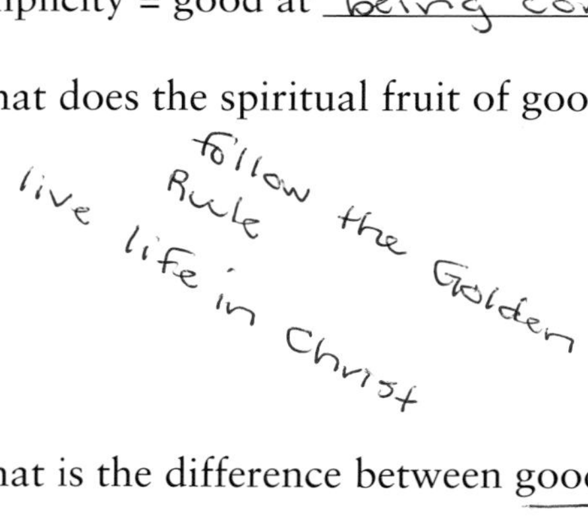

2. What is the difference between goodness and good deeds?

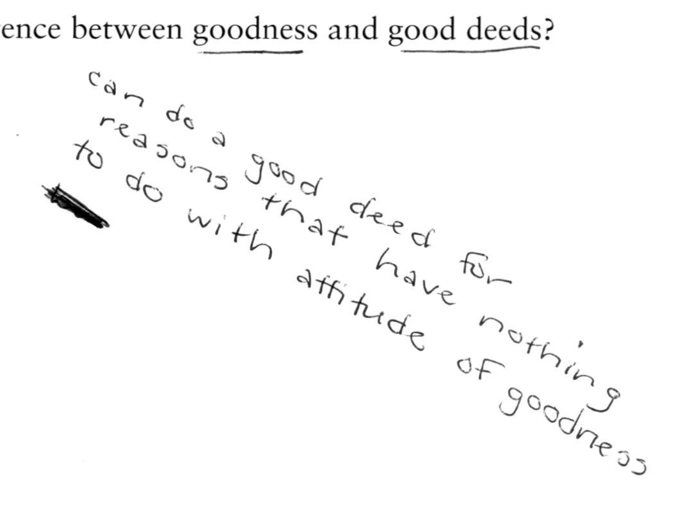

3. Jesus prized the simplicity, purity, and dependency of little children. What kinds of things may hold adults back from this?

innocence pride
inquisitive greed

4. How can being rich—in money, education, status, popularity, privilege—make it hard to "enter the kingdom of God" (Luke 18:25)?

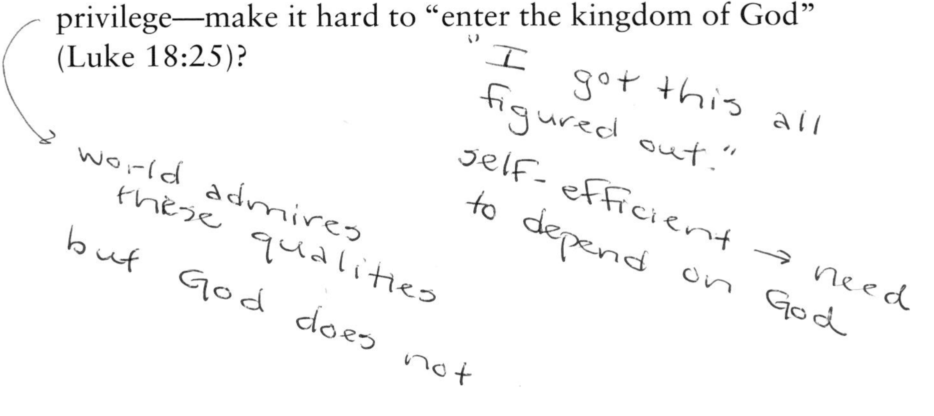

5. How important is it to you to be appreciated, thanked, or recognized for the good things you do?

not very - at the moment it's okay but don't need "likes"

6. What is one way you can do a completely secret good deed this week—and keep it secret?

Fruitful Activation

- Search the internet or scan a magazine for other ways we see the concept of goodness. What makes for good land? A good leader? A good experience? Use your imagination and see if any of your searches spark more understanding of what goodness might look like in different situations.
- Keep a journal this coming week. When you spend time with Jesus, ask him what you need to know and what you need to do about situations that are before you. Write these things in your journal and start getting into the habit of depending on Jesus. You might be surprised where this type of journaling takes you.
- Eat some chocolate! Make it a research project on the fruit of goodness. What makes good chocolate *good?* Read the labels and try several grades and kinds of chocolate, noting the differences in taste, texture, and quality, depending on what is added to the pure chocolate. After all, cacao is a fruit!

Notes

GENTLENESS & SELF-CONTROL

Inner Strengths

Gentleness & Self-Control

We've come to the last two spiritual fruits on Paul's list: gentleness and self-control. These may seem like opposites. It's easy to envision self-control as the "I am the master of my fate" feeling that drives us to dig in our heels and work harder to be better. (Paul might have called this "the flesh.") Conversely, gentleness might seem to be a passive, sweet, doormat-like quality. But nothing could be further from the truth! Webster's dictionary has defined self-control as "restraint exercised over oneself." From not eating the whole box of Girl Scout cookies to calmly responding to a verbal attack, self-control is a quiet strength that keeps us centered. Gentleness has been described as "sensitivity of disposition and kindness of behavior, founded on strength and prompted by love."[8]

Both fruits have to do with strength, not weakness. With self-control, it is strength over oneself and one's desires. Gentleness is a strength that keeps us from unkindness and insensitivity, so we can be peacemakers and solution-bringers—as opposed to people who fan the flames of anger and fear. There's no doormat-likeness here, but rather an inner strength that can step back from our own emotions and discern the best and most loving response in any situation.

Key Bible Passages

John 15:1–17 NT p. 101

Titus 2:1–15 NT p. 197

Optional Reading

Titus 1:5–9

1 Peter 3:8–22

“Better a patient person than a warrior, one with self-control than one who takes a city.”

PROVERBS 16:32

Know It

1. In John 15:1–17, Jesus describes the source for growing all spiritual fruit. What are some of the "fruits" mentioned or alluded to in this passage?

2. In Jesus' imagery of the vine and branches, what do you think are the branches that bear no fruit—and what becomes of them?

3. What are some reasons Paul gives in Titus 2:1–15 for Christians to live self-controlled lives?

Explore It

Flourishing Fruit

Some might call it maturity, that strength of not being swayed by the shouting and aggression of others. Certainly, it is the mature tree that bears fruit—a signifier of spiritual growth. Yet the paradox of this great strength is that it comes not by doing more or working harder, but through increasing dependence on Jesus: more resting in him, more asking him what he wants us to know, what he wants us to do, and more praise and thanksgiving! These factors will make us stronger than we can imagine in the ways that matter most. Just as Jesus said, "If you remain in me and I in you, you will bear much fruit" (John 15:5).

Can you see how this greater dependence on Jesus brings us full circle back to the fruits of love, joy, and peace? The fruit of God's Spirit is not a laundry list of saintly virtues, because virtues are things we're told to develop on our own and "do better" at

Self-Control

The Greek word for *self-control* in Galatians 5:23 is *egkrateia,* pronounced eg-KRAH-teh-ee-ah. Also translated as *temperance*, it means restraint. It and its variants occur less than ten times in the New Testament. Another common word used in the New Testament for self-control is *sophroneo,* which means "to be in one's right mind."

them. But in God's kingdom, it's in greater rest of soul and deeper dependence on God that we see the flourishing of spiritual fruit. And all these fruits are symbiotic. They work together and feed off one another as we "grow in the grace and the knowledge of our Lord Jesus Christ" (2 Peter 3:18).

Consider what the life cycle of a grapevine can teach us about growing spiritual fruit:

- Without a root, there is no fruit. There is no job for the branch to do, except to remain connected to the root stock, or in Jesus' words, the vine.
- This is a cultivated plant. It's the result of a series of processes that flow life and health into the branch. However, there are diseases, blights, and insect attacks that can cause the branch to no longer receive the flow of life from the vine and become withered.
- Spiritually speaking, sin can choke the branches of the vine. Sin is a turning away from Jesus, which brings shame, fear, and guilt. But then, as we repent and turn back to him, the flow of his life fills us, and we once again begin to produce the fruits of his Spirit.

Gentleness

The Greek word for *gentleness* in Galatians 5:23 is *prautes,* pronounced prah-OO-teys. In some Bible versions, this word is translated as *meekness* or *humility*. It signals a quiet spirit, the very opposite of arrogant pride. It occurs twelve times in the New Testament.

- Grapevines take years to grow to maturity. We often expect things to happen *right now*, but just as with grapevines, full fruitfulness doesn't come overnight. And spiritual fruit may take longer to grow than a cluster of grapes.

"Jesus never mistreated anyone just because they mistreated him. He confronted them in a spirit of gentleness and then continued to love them."

—JOYCE MEYER

In this study, we have focused not only on the fruits themselves—what those fruits look like and taste like—but also on *why* they grow, *who* supports the branches, and *how* the fruits flourish. In so many ways in Galatians 5, Paul urges believers to be in sync with the Holy Spirit: to "walk by the Spirit" (verse 16), be "led by the Spirit" (verse 18), "live by the Spirit" (verse 25), and "keep in step with the Spirit" (verse 25).

So how do we stay immersed in God's Spirit?

First, we must be aware that he is even there. If you're a believer in Jesus, then God's promise is that his Holy Spirit is within you (John 14:26).

Second, we keep short accounts with God. This means that we turn and ask forgiveness as soon as the Holy Spirit makes us aware of something we are doing wrong (1 John 1:7–9). We stay in a state of having a clear conscience—having, as one hymn writer put it, "Nothing between my soul and my Savior."

Third, we understand through Scripture, prayer, and other ways, that when God is asking us to do something, we simply obey. We don't try to figure it out or fix it on our own but ask him to tell us what we need to know and show us what we need to do. Otherwise, God's Spirit is grieved within us. When that's our state, the flow of spiritual life that we need gets tightened down. We start to live like cranky two-year-olds, trying to solve our own problems and spitting out nasty fruit on others: bitterness, rage, anger, brawling (Ephesians 4:29–32).

We've seen how self-effort is far less effective than Jesus' advice to "remain in me," and yet our self-help-oriented culture tells us that we can just do it and make ourselves better. This toxic mindset can be difficult for us to recognize because it's the air we breathe. We can easily quote a Bible verse and say we trust in the Lord with all our hearts and don't lean on our own understanding (Proverbs 3:5), but learning to humbly lean, to abide, and to remain in him instead of "fixing it myself" can be the hardest work of our lives. It's not something to do, but Someone we trust. In that process, God's Spirit challenges us to let go of our way, so that nothing blocks the full flow of his "sap" that flows from Jesus into us. That's what grows amazing spiritual fruits!

> "We must have a spirit of power towards the enemy, a spirit of love towards men, and a spirit of self-control towards ourselves."
>
> —WATCHMAN NEE

Life Application Questions

1. What do you think it means to *remain* or *abide* in Jesus the vine? stay closely – depend on Him

constant – continual
doing His will
He is everything we need
deep spiritual commitment

2. What are some typical human responses to stress and opposition—the "fruits of the flesh," as Paul might call them?
anger / short tempered
violence
drugs, alcohol, overindulgence
give up
frustration

3. What would self-controlled and gentle responses to stress and opposition look like? How can you demonstrate these fruits to others—even to strangers in the grocery store?

friendly
smile
patience

back off
deescalate
relax

think before speaking

4. What spiritual practices help you rest in and depend on Jesus?

prayer
read Bible
trust in God
praises & thanks

5. Looking back over all the fruits of God's Spirit, take some time to consider which ones seem to be the biggest and juiciest in your life. Circle those in the list below, then consider: Why did you choose those fruits?

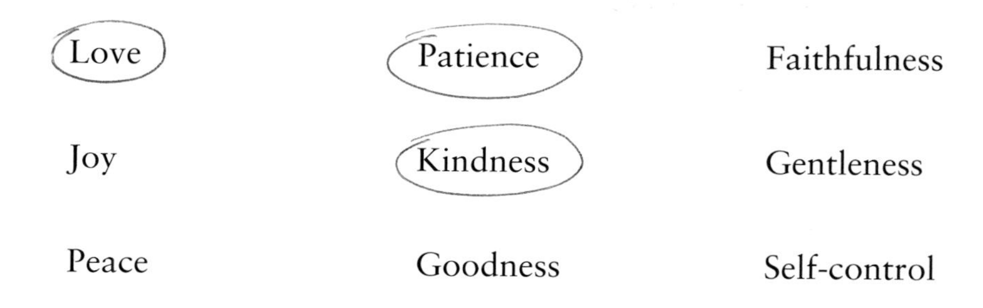

6. Which fruits didn't you circle—those fruits that seem a little puny in your life? Pray to God, asking him to grow these smaller fruits to maturity. And don't forget to thank God for all the fruit he is growing in you, even the ones just budding.

Fruitful Activation

- Having thought about how you best connect to and focus on Jesus, do a little research to find resources for that. Maybe it's time to read a new translation of the Bible or begin listening to God's Word from an audio Bible. The internet is full of possibilities, so ask Jesus what he wants you to access.
- Memorize Galatians 5:16–25. Break the passage into smaller units, turn it into a song, listen to it over and over, write each portion out on cards to place by your bathroom mirror. There are so many ways to learn it! The Holy Spirit will use what you commit to memory. As the psalm writer says, "I have hidden your word in my heart that I might not sin against you" (Psalm 119:11). There is power in knowing God's words because it helps us to keep the flow of God's Spirit unblocked.
- Engage your creative side. Creativity itself can be a way to remain or abide. Try one or more of these things: (1) Make a collage or painting that will remind you of what you learned in this study which you don't want to forget. Do it just for yourself. It doesn't need to be fancy art; it need not go on the wall, but it may, as a good reminder. (2) Draw a diagram or a picture of how the Holy Spirit (the sap) best flows from Jesus (the vine or rootstock) into you (the branch). It doesn't have to be a grapevine; maybe you're a mango tree! (3) Color the fruit of the Spirit art on the following page. Take your time and reflect on each of the fruits of the Spirit as you go.

PATIENCE
GOODNESS
Self-
control
LOVE
Faithfulness
KINDNESS
GENTLENESS
Joy
PEACE

Notes

Notes

"Encourage one another and build each other up."

1 THESSALONIANS 5:11

Leader's Guide

Congratulations! You've either decided to lead a Bible study, or you're thinking hard about it. Guess what? God does big things through small groups. When his people gather together, open his Word, and invite his Spirit to work, their lives are changed!

Do you feel intimidated yet?

Be comforted by this: even the great apostle Paul felt "in over his head" at times. When he went to Corinth to help people grasp God's truth, he admitted he was overwhelmed: "I came to you in weakness with great fear and trembling" (1 Corinthians 2:3). Later he wondered, "Who is adequate for such a task as this?" (2 Corinthians 2:16 NLT).

Feelings of inadequacy are normal; every leader has them. What's more, they're actually healthy. They keep us dependent on the Lord. It is in our times of greatest weakness that God works most powerfully. The Lord assured Paul, "My grace is sufficient for you, for my power is made perfect in weakness" (2 Corinthians 12:9).

The Goal

What is the goal of a Bible study group? Listen as the apostle Paul speaks to Christians:

- "Oh, my dear children! I feel as if I'm going through labor pains for you again, and they will continue until *Christ is fully developed in your lives*" (Galatians 4:19 NLT, emphasis added).
- "For God knew his people in advance, and he chose them *to become like his Son*" (Romans 8:29 NLT, emphasis added).

Do you see it? God's ultimate goal for us is that we would become like Jesus Christ. This means a Bible study is not about filling our heads with more information. Rather, it is about undergoing transformation. We study and apply God's truth so that it will reshape our hearts and minds, and so that over time, we will become more and more like Jesus.

Paul said, "The purpose of my instruction is that all believers would be filled with love that comes from a pure heart, a clear conscience, and genuine faith" (1 Timothy 1:5 NLT).

This isn't about trying to "master the Bible." No, we're praying that God's Word will master us, and through humble submission to its authority, we'll be changed from the inside out.

Your Role

Many group leaders experience frustration because they confuse their role with God's role. Here's the truth: God alone knows our deep hang-ups and hurts. Only he can save a soul, heal a heart, fix a life. It is God who rescues people from depression, addictions, bitterness, guilt, and shame. We Bible study leaders need to realize that *we can't do any of those things.*

So what can we do? More than we think!

- We can pray.
- We can trust God to work powerfully.
- We can obey the Spirit's promptings.
- We can prepare for group gatherings.
- We can keep showing up faithfully.

With group members:

- We can invite, remind, encourage, and love.
- We can ask good questions and then listen attentively.
- We can gently speak tough truths.
- We can celebrate with those who are happy and weep with those who are sad.
- We can call and text and let them know we've got their back.

But we can never do the things that only the Almighty can do.

- We can't play the Holy Spirit in another person's life.
- We can't be in charge of outcomes.
- We can't force God to work according to our timetables.

And one more important reminder: besides God's role and our role, group members also have a key role to play in this process. If they don't show up, prepare, or open their hearts to God's transforming truth, no life change will take place. We're not called to manipulate or shame, pressure or arm twist. We're not to blame if members don't make progress—and we don't get the credit when they do. We're mere instruments in the hands of God.

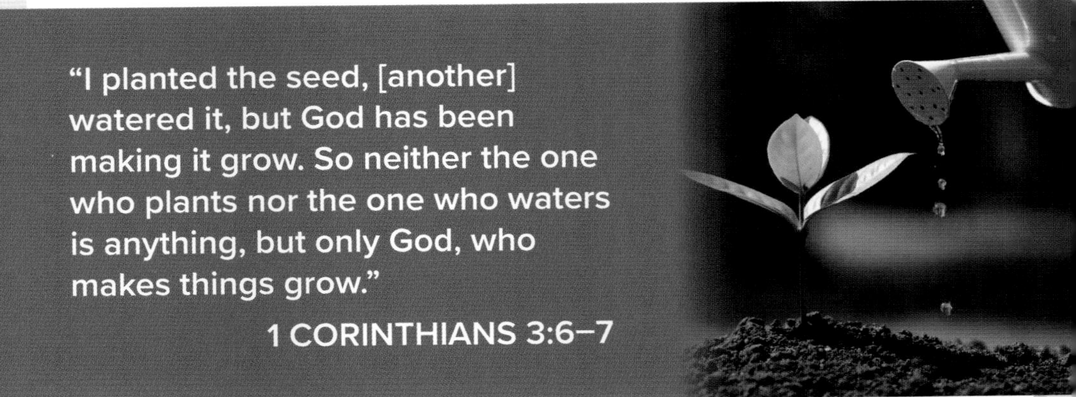

Leader Myths and Truths

Many people assume that a Bible study leader should:

- Be a Bible scholar.
- Be a dynamic communicator.
- Have a big, fancy house to meet in.
- Have it all together—no doubts, bad habits, or struggles.

These are myths—even outright lies of the enemy!

Here's the truth:

- God is looking for humble Bible students, not scholars.
- You're not signing up to give lectures, you're agreeing to facilitate discussions.
- You don't need a palace, just a place where you can have uninterrupted discussions. (Perhaps one of your group members will agree to host your study.)
- Nobody has it all together. We are all in process. We are all seeking to work out "our salvation with fear and trembling" (Philippians 2:12).

As long as your desire is that Jesus be Lord of your life, God will use you!

Some Bad Reasons to Lead a Group

- You want to wow others with your biblical knowledge.

  "Love . . . does not boast, it is not proud" (1 Corinthians 13:4).

- You're seeking a hidden personal gain or profit.

  "We do not peddle the word of God for profit" (2 Corinthians 2:17).

- You want to tell people how wrong they are.

  "Do not condemn" (Luke 6:37).

- You want to fix or rescue people.

  "It is God who works in you to will and to act" (Philippians 2:13).

- You're being pressured to do it.

  "Am I now trying to win the approval of human beings, or of God?" (Galatians 1:10).

A Few Do's

✔ Pray for your group.

Are you praying for your group members regularly? It is the most important thing a leader can do for his or her group.

✔ Ask for help.

If you're new at leading, spend time with an experienced group leader and pick his or her brain.

✔ Encourage members to prepare.

Challenge participants to read the Bible passages and the material in their study guides, and to answer and reflect on the study questions during the week prior to meeting.

✔ Discuss the group guidelines.

Go over important guidelines with your group at the first session, and again as needed if new members join the group in later sessions. See the *Group Guidelines* at the end of this leader's guide.

✔ Share the load.

Don't be a one-person show. Ask for volunteers. Let group members host the meeting, arrange for snacks, plan socials, lead group prayer times, and so forth. The old saying is true: Participants become boosters; spectators become critics.

✔ Be flexible.

If a group member shows up in crisis, it is okay to stop and take time to surround the hurting brother or sister with love. Provide a safe place for sharing. Listen and pray for his or her needs.

✔ Be kind.

Remember, there's a story—often a heart-breaking one—behind every face. This doesn't *excuse* bad or disruptive behavior on the part of group members, but it might *explain* it.

A Few Don'ts

✘ Don't "wing it."

Although these sessions are designed to require minimum preparation, read each one ahead of time. Highlight the questions you feel are especially important for your group to spend time on.

✘ Don't feel ashamed to say, "I don't know."

Disciple means "learner," not "know-it-all."

✘ Don't feel the need to "dump the truck."

You don't have to say everything you know. There is always next week. A little silence during group discussion time, that's fine. Let members wrestle with questions.

✘ Don't put members on the spot.

Invite others to share and pray, but don't pressure them. Give everyone an opportunity to participate. People will open up on their own time as they learn to trust the group.

✘ Don't go down "rabbit trails."

Be careful not to let one person dominate the time or for the discussion to go down the gossip road. At the same time, don't short-circuit those occasions when the Holy Spirit is working in your group members' lives and therefore they *need* to share a lot.

✘ Don't feel pressure to cover every question.

Better to have a robust discussion of four questions than a superficial conversation of ten.

✘ Don't go long.

Encourage good discussion, but don't be afraid to "rope 'em back in" when needed. Start and end on time. If you do this from the beginning, you'll avoid the tendency of group members to arrive later and later as the season goes on.

How to Use This Study Guide

Many group members have busy lives—dealing with long work hours, childcare, and a host of other obligations. These sessions are designed to be as simple and straightforward as possible to fit into a busy schedule. Nevertheless, encourage group members to set aside some time during the week (even if it's only a little) to pray, read the key Bible passage, and respond to questions in this study guide. This will make the group discussion and experience much more rewarding for everyone.

Each session contains four parts.

Read It

The *Key Bible Passage* is the portion of Scripture everyone should read during the week before the group meeting. The group can read it together at the beginning of the session as well.

The *Optional Reading* is for those who want to dig deeper and read lengthier Bible passages on their own during the week.

Know It

This section encourages participants to reflect on the Bible passage they've just read. Here, the goal is to interact with the biblical text and grasp what it says. (We'll get into practical application later.)

Explore It

Here group members can find background information with charts and visuals to help them understand the Bible passage and the topic more deeply. They'll move beyond the text itself and see how it connects to other parts of Scripture and the historical and cultural context.

Live It

Finally, participants will examine how God's Word connects to their lives. There are application questions for group discussion or personal reflection, practical ideas to apply what they've learned from God's Word, and a closing thought and/or prayer. (Remember, you don't have to cover all the questions or everything in this section during group time. Focus on what's most important for your group.)

Celebrate!

Here's an idea: Have a plan for celebrating your time together after the last session of this Bible study. Do something special after your gathering time, or plan a separate celebration for another time and place. Maybe someone in your group has the gift of hospitality—let them use their gifting and organize the celebration.

	30-MINUTE SESSION	60-MINUTE SESSION
READ IT	Open in prayer and read the *Key Bible Passage.* 5 minutes	Open in prayer and read the *Key Bible Passage.* 5 minutes
KNOW IT	Ask: "What stood out to you from this Bible passage?" 5 minutes	Ask: "What stood out to you from this Bible passage?" 5 minutes
EXPLORE IT	Encourage group members to read this section on their own, but don't spend group time on it. Move on to the life application questions.	Ask: "What did you find new or helpful in the *Explore It* section? What do you still have questions about?" 10 minutes
LIVE IT	Members voluntarily share their answers to 3 or 4 of the life application questions. 15 minutes	Members voluntarily share their answers to the life application questions. 25 minutes
PRAYER & CLOSING	Conclude with a brief prayer. 5 minutes	Share prayer requests and praise reports. Encourage the group to pray for each other in the coming week. Conclude with a brief prayer. 15 minutes

	90-MINUTE SESSION
	Open in prayer and read the *Key Bible Passage.* 5 minutes
	• Ask: "What stood out to you from this Bible passage?" • Then go over the *Know It* questions as a group. 10 minutes
	• Ask: "What did you find new or helpful in the *Explore It* section? What do you still have questions about?" • Here, the leader can add information found while preparing for the session. • If there are questions or a worksheet in this section, go over those as a group. 20 minutes
	• Members voluntarily share their answers to the life application questions. • Wrap up this time with a closing thought or suggestions for how to put into practice in the coming week what was just learned from God's Word. 30 minutes
	• Share prayer requests and praise reports. • Members voluntarily pray during group time about the requests and praises shared. • Encourage the group to pray for each other in the coming week. 25 minutes

Group Guidelines

This group is about discovering God's truth, supporting each other, and finding growth in our new life in Christ. To reach these goals, a group needs a few simple guidelines that everyone should follow for the group to stay healthy and for trust to develop.

1. **Everyone agrees to make group time a priority.**
   We understand that there are work, health, and family issues that come up. So if there is an emergency or schedule conflict that cannot be avoided, be sure to let someone know that you can't make it that week. This may seem like a small thing, but it makes a big difference to your other group members.
2. **What is said in the group stays in the group.**
   Accept it now: we are going to share some personal things. Therefore, the group must be a safe and confidential place to share.
3. **Don't be judgmental, even if you strongly disagree.**
   Listen first, and contribute your perspective only as needed. Remember, you don't fully know someone else's story. Take this advice from James: "Be quick to listen, slow to speak, and slow to become angry" (James 1:19).
4. **Be patient with one another.**
   We are all in process, and some of us are hurting and struggling more than others. Don't expect bad habits or attitudes to disappear overnight.
5. **Everyone participates.**
   It may take time to learn how to share, but as you develop a trust toward the other group members, take the chance.

If you struggle in any of these areas, ask God's help for growth, and ask the group to help hold you accountable. Remember, you're all growing together.

Notes

Notes

Endnotes

1 All Webster's dictionary definitions in this book are from Webster's Dictionary 1927 edition (G. & C. Merriam Co, 1927).

2 All definitions for Greek words in this book are based on the *Expository Dictionary of Bible Words,* ed. Stephen D. Renn (Peabody, MA: Hendrickson Publishers, 2005).

3 Cornelius Plantinga, *Not the Way It's Supposed to Be: A Breviary of Sin* (Grand Rapids: Eerdmans, 1996), 10.

4 Oswald Chambers, *My Utmost for His Highest,* January 25 and April 29 entries.

5 Henri J. M. Nouwen, *Bread for the Journey: A Daybook of Wisdom and Faith* (HarperCollins, 2006), January 5 entry.

6 Thomas Merton, *Disputed Questions* (Harvest Books, 1985), 125.

7 This quote is widely attributed to John Wesley, but it's doubtful he actually said it; nonetheless, it's still a *good* quote.

8 *Baker's Evangelical Dictionary of Theology,* ed. Walter A. Elwell (Grand Rapids: Baker Book House Company, 1996), s. v. "Gentleness."

ROSE VISUAL BIBLE STUDIES

6-Session Study Guides for Personal or Group Use

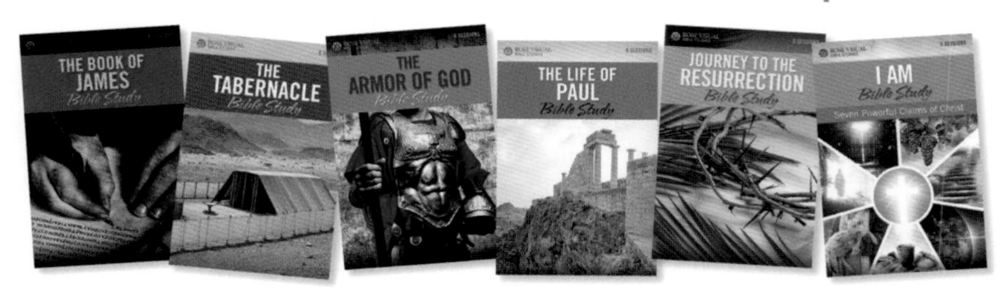

THE BOOK OF JAMES
Find out how to cultivate a living faith through six tests of faith.

THE TABERNACLE
Discover how each item of the tabernacle foreshadowed Jesus.

THE ARMOR OF GOD
Dig deep into Ephesians 6 and learn the meaning of each piece of the armor.

THE LIFE OF PAUL
See how the apostle Paul persevered through trials and proclaimed the gospel.

JOURNEY TO THE RESURRECTION
Renew your heart and mind as you engage in spiritual practices. Perfect for Easter.

I AM
Know the seven powerful claims of Christ from the gospel of John.

THE TWELVE DISCIPLES
Learn about the twelve men Jesus chose to be his disciples.

PROVERBS
Gain practical, godly wisdom from the book of Proverbs.

WOMEN OF THE BIBLE: OLD TESTAMENT
Journey through six inspiring stories of women of courage and wisdom.

WOMEN OF THE BIBLE: NEW TESTAMENT
See women's impact in the ministry of Jesus and the early church.

THE LORD'S PRAYER
Deepen your prayer life with the seven petitions in the Lord's Prayer.

FRUIT OF THE SPIRIT
Explore the nine spiritual fruits.

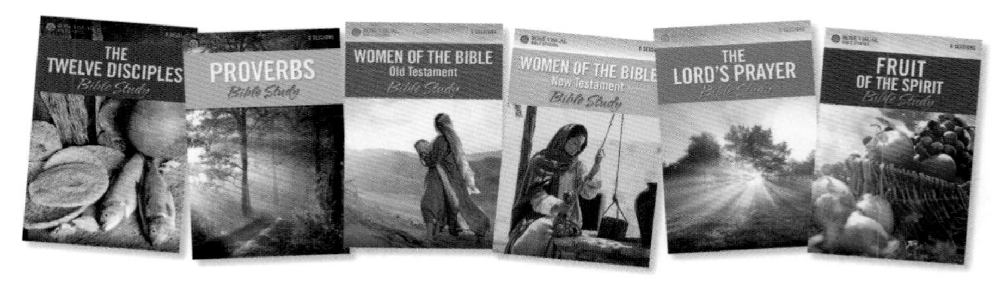

www.hendricksonrose.com